PLAY IT AGAIN, CHESTER

VOLUME ONE

BOOGIES, RAGS AND BLUES FOR PIANO

MUSIC BY
CAROL BARRATT

Chester Music
(A Music Sales Limited Company)
8/9 Frith Street, London W1V 5TZ
Exclusive distributors: Music Sales Ltd., Newmarket Road,
Bury St. Edmunds, Suffolk IP33 3YB

Six Technical Tips

The syncopated rhythms have the counts underneath.

Used on page 3

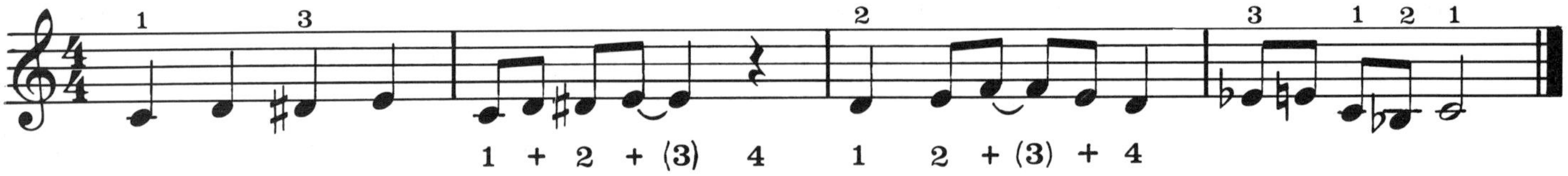

Used on page 6

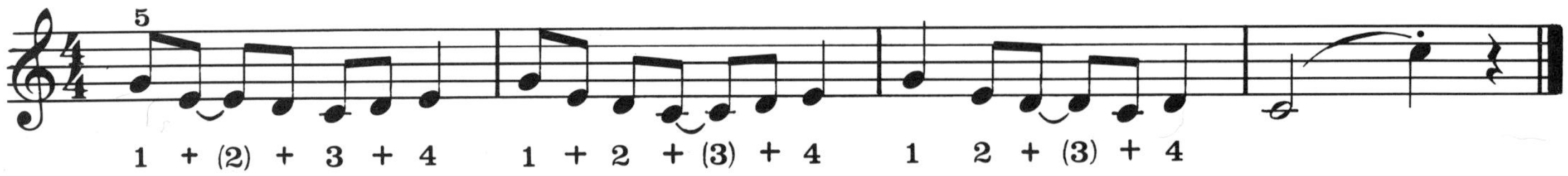

Used on page 7

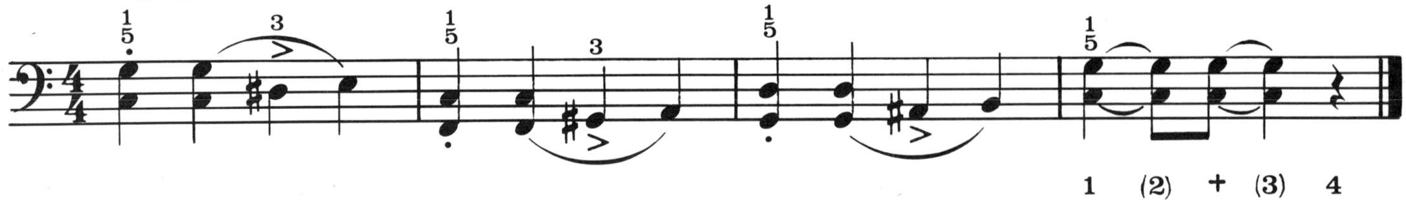

Used on page 8

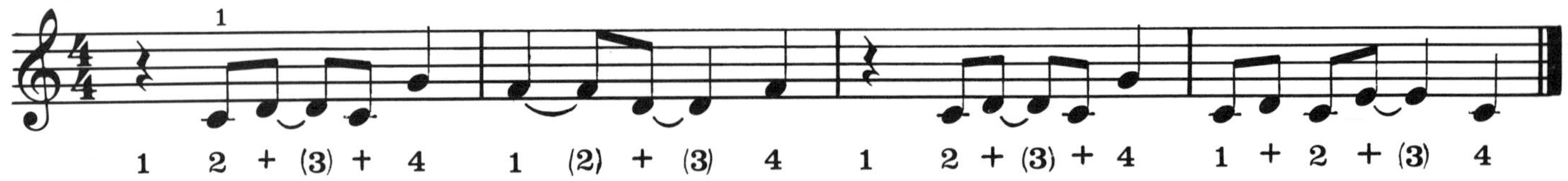

Used on page 12

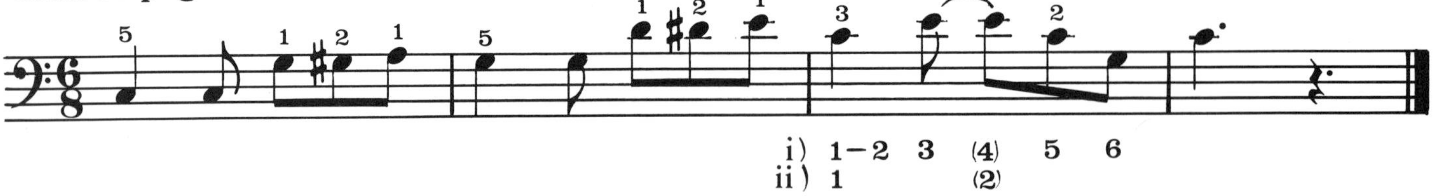

Used on page 15

NAVY BLUES

CHEESE-CAKE-WALK

OUT OF STEP

RIPSTITCH RAG

HONKY-TONK STOMP

Very bouncy

LAZY HAZE

BUTTERFINGER BOOGIE

With a steady beat

MACDONALD'S PLACE

OUT TO LUNCH

BOBBY SHAFTOE'S SHUFFLE

mp
mf
f

BLUE WALTZ

BEANERY BOOGIE

CODA

Add the last two chords yourself!

Reproduced and printed by
Halstan & Co. Ltd., Amersham, Bucks., England